Bibliographic information of the German National Library:
The German National Library lists this publication in the German National
Bibliography; detailed bibliographic data is available
on the Internet at dnb.dnb.de.

© 2025 Regina Toedter. Translated from the German
with the original title "Zuckersucht-Killer. Die 50 besten Tipps"
Publisher: BoD · Books on Demand GmbH, In de Tarpen 42,
22848 Norderstedt, bod@bod.de
Print: Libri Plureos GmbH, Friedensallee 273, 22763 Hamburg.

2015 Original edition published by Trias Verlag Stuttgart by MVS
Medizinverlage Stuttgart GmbH & Co.KG. (Germany).

ISBN: 978-3-7693-5218-4

Sugar-free recipes pp 53-61: Healthy snacking can be so easy. All the products featured here are homemade and guaranteed to contain no (industrial) sugar. Alternatives include xylitol, stevia or pureed/ chopped dates.

Zero sugar. The 50 best tips

by Regina Toedter

About the book

Let's face it: your morning cereal tastes better when it's soaked in sweet chocolate milk, your office snack drawer is well stocked, and when your local pastry chef conjures up such delicious treats, you should reward them. Reaching for a sweet treat is simply more tempting than reaching for the veggie sticks. It's just a shame that over the course of the day it can add up to more sugar than is good for us. This little helper shows you how to control your sweet tooth without depriving yourself: **Zero sugar. 50 simple tips** to fit into your daily routine. Just pick what you like, get started and enjoy everyday life without the temptation of sweetness.

About the author

Author **Regina Toedter** knows the challenge of sugar addiction from her own experience. As a child, she sometimes preferred to spend her pocket money on sweets, and as a teenager she even skipped whole meals in favour of snacks. These habits left her feeling tired and unable to concentrate. It was not until she was 25, 15 years ago, that she decided to make a radical change to her sugar intake. Today she is off sugar, five kilos lighter and two dress sizes smaller. Even better, she no longer has to deal with unpleasant visits to the dentist and the typical afternoon slump is a thing of the past. Regina Toedter's positive experience has inspired many people to take a closer look at their own sugar consumption. She helps others with valuable insights and strategies for a more conscious approach to sugar.

More books by the author

Alcohol-free. The best tips (2024)
Fun Running (2024)
Holistay. How I travel at home to always be on holiday (2019)

You can also read Regina Toedter´s health column
in FOCUS magazine.

Regina Toedter

Zero sugar

The 50 best tips

Content

Foreword

Dear Reader,

We've all been there: at some point during the day we get a craving for something sweet. The thought of that fragrant chocolate croissant at the baker's in the morning or the chocolates in our desk drawer suddenly hits us. This is completely normal and can be explained in simple biological terms: The blood sugar level in the body drops after gradual consumption and the energy in the body dwindles. However, there are now 24 hours in a day and the brain is increasingly signalling the need for new energy in the form of carbohydrates, mainly from foods such as bread, pasta, fruit or even sweets. The more complex the sugar or carbohydrate molecules in a food (such as whole grains), the slower they are broken down by the body and the longer the body can use them. The industrial sugars used in sweets, on the other hand, are so-called empty carbohydrates, which means they contain virtually no vitamins and minerals, are digested quickly and are absorbed quickly into the bloodstream. This is why jelly babies, chocolate bars and the like cause our blood sugar levels to rise very fast and then fall again very quickly. The result: after a brief energy boost, the body soon needs a glucose refill. This is how the craving for sweets comes about.

It is always a balancing act to know when and how many carbohydrates we need. Some people seem to get it right. They seem to be able to eat everything and snack endlessly without gaining weight or having problems. Their bodies process sugar perfectly. How do they do it? It all depends on how much you eat, when you eat it and, of course, your individual digestion. So why do so many people fail to properly assess their actual energy needs? Why do we eat more and more industrially produced sugar, with the result that we feel unwell or even sick?

One of the reasons for this is undoubtedly that in today's age of abundance, all kinds of food are constantly available to us. Sweets, which kept our Stone Age ancestors alive as a quick source of energy in the form of berries and fruits, are now available in abundance - usually quite high in sugar. And we eat far too much of it at the wrong time. Sugar is everywhere! We now know that it goes by many names (sucrose, dextrose, fructose, molasses, etc.) and likes to disguise itself as a carbohydrate on food labels. Our bodies are addicted to it. And why not? Carbohydrates are the ultimate energy source. But when we consume them, especially in the form of (industrial) sugar, our blood sugar levels go into overdrive - with fatal consequences. The processing of sugary foods in the quantities we consume puts our bodies at long-term risk of disease. We now know the effects: Tooth decay, obesity, high blood pressure, cardiovascular problems, diabetes, osteoporosis and infectious diseases. Unfortunately, most people do not realise this until it is almost too late. So why wait for the doctor?

Sugar has addictive potential

The craving for sweets is not usually described as a typical dependency or addiction in the medical sense, but more and more scientific studies are pointing to the strong link between sugar consumption and addictive behaviour. Such behaviour occurs when we feel we cannot do without something and become mentally and/or physically dependent on a stimulant or activity, be it alcohol, nicotine, internet gaming or shopping.

The line between regular, everyday using and becoming addicted is often blurred. However, as soon as we notice that we are already showing compulsive behaviour, i.e. that we need to consume more and more, cannot stop and suffer from withdrawal symptoms, loss of control and listlessness when we stop, the red flags should go up. Although sugar is not a dangerous drug, we all know that excessive consumption of sweets can lead to addictive behaviour and, as we know, can be harmful to our health in the long term.

But what happens in our brains when we eat sugar? Our body's reward system releases the happiness hormone dopamine every time we eat sugar, giving us a feeling of satisfaction and euphoria. Over time, however, the body becomes accustomed to this state. When the quick energy boost from sweets is taken away, our mood deteriorates. We become irritable and moody. Our reward system becomes unbalanced, which can have a negative effect on our motivation and impulse control. This means that our cravings become stronger than our willpower: we can no longer resist sweets. You can find out if you are prone to sugar addiction by taking a short self-test in the appendix of this book.

How can we avoid industrial sugar? Sweet foods provide readily available fuel for our bodies, which we need especially when we are doing a lot of mental work and exercising. But instead of choosing healthy carbohydrate-rich foods, we often consume the wrong kind of sugar, namely industrial sugar, and usually in excessive amounts. We need to find new ways to change not only our diet but also some of our lifestyle habits to avoid falling into the sweet trap in the future.

The good news is that you already have a guide! In this book you will find 50 good tips to help you curb and control your sweet tooth using simple methods. All you need is curiosity, fun and a little patience with yourself and your body.

The book is divided into three categories: The first focuses on ourselves. It discusses the internal and external causes of our sweet tooth and how you can personalise your sugar-free lifestyle. The second group focuses on our environment: how do social norms, social consensus or our upbringing influence our sugar addiction? The tips listed here will help you to break old habits and also allow those around you to share in the positive aspects of your dietary change. We need new, interesting and inspiring ways to beat sugar addiction for good! These will be presented in the final group.

All the tips and tricks can be easily integrated into your everyday life and are easy to implement. You will see that cutting out (industrial) sugar is not that difficult - and the rewards will not be long in coming: you will feel much fitter, healthier and happier in no time at all.

It's best to start today!
I wish you lots of fun and success,

Regina Toedter

Simply get started

Want to get rid of your sweet tooth? Be happy - you have already taken the most important step.

Some things are easier to do spontaneously and from the gut than to plan in advance. The formula is simple: learn by doing, just start and try. This is how this guide is designed. Let your intention be followed by action. With your first successes, you will start a real chain reaction and enjoy the process more and more! So start enriching your life today by overcoming your sugar addiction with simple strategies. Despite the quick successes, do not be too impatient at first. Lasting habit change takes time. Treat every task as a challenge and every initial failure as an opportunity. In this section you will learn to look closely: from the ingredients list to the supermarket shelf to the fridge compartment. But your other senses, your awareness and your physical fitness will also be actively challenged! With humour and spice, you will finally banish those pesky sugar cravings from your everyday life. So what are you waiting for? Just do it!

1 Dust off

Nothing feels better than that first feeling of success. And you can have it right now: Look in your fridge and play detective. Banish all sugary foods from your kitchen and make your local charity happy. Start today and your health will thank you! Do you find it hard to give food away? Do it this once and know that you are taking the fight against your sugar addiction seriously. A non-smoker going through withdrawal doesn't hide cigarettes in a drawer, the temptation is too great. Don't put yourself through this ordeal. Watch out for hidden sugar, for example in sausages, ketchup or sauces. It can also be found in frozen pizzas, ready-made salads, canned vegetables, juices, soya milk, cornflakes, cereals, white bread and fruit yoghurts. Don't forget your pantry, office drawers and secret stashes. When you give these surplus foods away and they are no longer on your shopping list, you will have achieved your first goal: healthier shopping and therefore healthier living. Do this again and again and make it a ritual. You will be amazed at how stubbornly hidden sugar continues to creep into your household.

2 Shop and cook consciously

What are you going to eat? Your fridge and kitchen shelves may suddenly be completely empty. But you won't starve! Now is the time to make a list of recommended foods and stick to it. What can you eat with a clear conscience? A simple rule applies: The more natural the food, the better for your health. At first, you may feel a bit disoriented when you walk through the supermarket. Vegetables, whole grains, fruit, herbs, meat, oils and nuts are all right and important. However, be careful when buying sweet fruit, juices and dried fruit. These foods are known to be high in fructose and should only be consumed in moderation, even though they should be included in your diet for their high content of important vitamins, minerals and trace elements. You should also take a close look at meat. Buy only fresh, untreated meat (preferably organic) and avoid marinated, pickled and prepared products. After a short time, you will automatically go to the right shelves and pick the right products. No more nougat cream sneaking up on you.

And how about eating out less and cooking more? Maybe you'll also need to tidy up your wardrobe. Because changing your diet will automatically help you shed a few extra pounds: you can look forward to your new feel-good size and your next shopping trip!

Extra tip

Your next shopping list should include 3 types of vegetables, 2 types of fruit, (sweet) potatoes, brown rice, 1 bulb of ginger, fresh herbs and spices, nuts, almonds, linseed meal, oatmeal, cocoa (100%), organic milk (even better hazelnut or almond milk), eggs, linseed oil, 1 piece of (organic) meat or fish, mushrooms, buckwheat, wholemeal bread, pulses, possibly soya products, hard cheese, natural yoghurt, herbal and green tea.

3 Sweet alternatives: what are they?

Natural sweeteners such as maple syrup, (wildflower) honey, coconut blossom sugar or agave syrup can be alternatives to sugar. They are rich in minerals, but they can be very fattening and can damage your teeth. Sugar substitutes such as isomalt, maltitol, lactitol, erythritol or xylitol are chemical in nature and often have unpleasant side effects such as bloating and diarrhoea if consumed in excess. However, they are ideal for baking cakes and biscuits. Xylitol, for example, not only has 40 per cent fewer calories than conventional industrial sugar, it also prevents tooth decay and has a low impact on blood sugar levels. Xylitol is derived from birch bark. Stevia, a sweetener derived from the stevia plant, can also be used in desserts and baking. Although the sweetener sometimes has a slightly bitter aftertaste that takes some getting used to, it contains no calories and does not cause tooth decay.

However, caution is advised with many stevia products: Chocolate bars, candies, jams and syrups often contain sugar as well as stevia. Another healthy alternative is dried or fresh fruit, which is also ideal for preparing sweet dishes. Thanks to their fibre, they'll fill you up quickly and won't make you overeat. For example, cut dried dates into small pieces and mix them with plain yoghurt. Sliced bananas or a handful of fresh raspberries with vanilla or cocoa are also great for a sweet dessert and can even be frozen and used as a substitute for ice cream.

Extra tip

- Sweet alternatives for breakfast: plain yoghurt; homemade rice pudding with cinnamon, cocoa and vanilla; berries or sliced fruit (apple, kiwi or pear)
- Snack when stressed: nuts, bananas, avocado, radishes, cherry tomatoes or cashew-cranberry mix
- Dessert after a hearty lunch: sugar-free chocolate shake, cheese sticks or soy drink
- Afternoon coffee: a handful of dried fruit
- Snack in front of the TV: sliced vegetables
- At the cinema: grapes or a 99% cocoa chocolate bar
- At the next party: homemade honey cake or xylitol cookies
- At parties: exotic fruit such as papaya, pineapple, mango, lychee or physalis
- To take to work: fruit basket, nut bread or herb power bread

What is your sweet favourite? If you like your coffee sweetened, try lactose-free milk next time. Thanks to a special treatment, it is sweeter than regular milk and a wonderful substitute for a spoonful of sugar.

4 Decoding of the ingredient list

Look at the list of ingredients on every product you buy. What does it say and what does it really contain? A 'sugar free' label is no guarantee that the product is sugar free. In most cases, a sugar-free label on the packaging is already suspect. Sugar is hidden behind names like sucrose, fructose, glucose syrup, mannose, maltose, dextrose, lactose, cornstarch, maltodextrin and many more. So why does sugar have so many different names? It's simple: the ingredient that's present in the largest amount in the product is always listed first.

As a result, sugar is often at the top of the list for many ready meals and confectionery products, which can put consumers off buying them. That's why creative food manufacturers like to dip into their bag of tricks: They list sugar under different names. That way, it's not immediately obvious. There is now a food traffic light system (Nutri-Score) to help consumers better assess the nutritional value of a product. The emphasis is on "supposedly" because the score does not take into account value-adding ingredients such as vitamins, minerals or unsaturated fatty acids, nor additives such as flavour enhancers, sweeteners or flavourings.

What is critical is that the fat content is taken as the benchmark and sugar is treated rather leniently. As we now know, fat is not the problem. Choosing the right healthy fats, such as vegetable oils from flaxseed, nuts, sesame, avocado or fish, and using them sparingly, is healthier than the fat-free but sugary foods that the Nutroscore incorrectly suggests. So when you shop, look for foods with a short list of ingredients or, better still, no list at all.

5 `Who is nibbling at my house?'

Everyone knows the German fairy tale of Hansel and Gretel who get lost in the woods and are lured by the wicked witch's crunchy house. Unfortunately, in our everyday world, this crunchy house is not hidden in the deep, deep forest, but on every street corner. There is no avoiding it, and the temptation to nibble is great. A biscuit here, a piece of cake there, always something sweet in between. That's why we need a plan: we don't have to go as far as trying to get rid of the witch somehow, but we can learn to give her a wide berth in the first place. If we know that the bakery will drive us mad with its fresh chocolate croissants every morning, we will avoid that route and try another. After all, we can get our latte macchiato somewhere else. Avoid places that make you feel weak: the bakery, the kiosk or the ice-cream parlour. Don't even go to the sweets aisle in the supermarket and consciously focus on other things at the checkout, such as the product selection of the people in front of you or behind you. Be happy that you can do without many of these items or be inspired by other healthy options. In this way you will create new habits and eventually you will not even notice the crispy treats.

6 Do not always follow your nose

Do you think about sweets all the time? Sure - because your nose is constantly reminded! It starts in the morning in the shower, when you're not even awake: As you lather your hair with shampoo, you may be hit by the pleasant scent of sweet strawberries. Hand soap smells like sweet apples, lip balm tastes like cherries and deodorant smells like delicate vanilla. So it's no wonder you're craving a sweet biscuit with your freshly ground coffee for breakfast. Outside the home, too, you are constantly tempted by scents.

Shops have long used specific olfactory stimuli to influence our emotions. Everywhere we go, we encounter a multitude of fragrant scents. We are subconsciously encouraged to buy products because the scents around us have a harmonising and seductive effect on us, and we associate them with pleasant feelings and experiences. So it's no wonder that we always have a craving for sweets. Even small changes can help: Reduce odours by choosing fragrance-free products. And never go to the shops hungry.

7 See the beautiful

Franz Kafka once said: 'Those who retain the ability to recognise beauty never grow old'. Recognise the beauty in yourself and your surroundings: it often helps to look at a picture of yourself from a time when you were visibly happy, beautiful and slim. That's where you want to be again!

It doesn't have to be a photo of yourself, sometimes you discover great images and illustrations while flipping through your favourite magazine. It doesn't matter what it is. The main thing is that it should be something that you particularly like and that arouses a burning desire in you: a breathtaking natural landscape (in which you see yourself jogging, for example), a great outfit (presented by a model with a great figure, of course) or a person you admire for something very specific.

You are bound to linger for a few seconds and feel a little wanderlust. Cut out the photo and hang it prominently over your desk, even framed if you like. It will remind you every day of that perfect place, that great figure or that admirable personality. The perfect motivation to do something yourself to get closer to your ideal. From now on, you will think twice before going back to the fridge and giving in to your sugar addiction. You will look for nicer places in your neighbourhood and take better care of yourself. And to make sure the picture doesn't get lost in the mundane, you'll swap it for other beautiful images from time to time.

8 Beware of alcohol traps!

Alcohol not only dulls the senses, it also makes you hungry. It's all too easy to reach for an unhealthy snack over a glass of wine and stop thinking about what healthy food you could be eating. It's easy to reach for the nearest bag of jelly babies or bowl of crisps.

When you're out and about and suddenly feel a little hungry, you're likely to head for the nearest takeaway, petrol station or kiosk. Without much thought, you grab a burger, kebab or chocolate bar. Your good intentions may have been forgotten, you just want to have fun that night and not worry about carbohydrates and calories! So if you're going out and you know you're going to drink alcohol: Eat your fill beforehand, pack a small healthy snack and remember to drink plenty of water. If you do end up in a snack bar after a fun night out with friends, enjoy the evening - knowing that it is an exception.

9 Just run away

Do as our ancestors did: Get moving! Move yourself and those around you. Whenever and as often as you can:

on your way to work, to the shops or in your spare time. Walk, run, swim, cycle - whatever the sport, be active! If you can get at least three hours of active exercise a week, you are well on your way to kicking your sugar habit. Take every flight of stairs, exercise your muscles and work on your flexibility. Exercise stimulates the metabolism and creates a natural balance between energy expenditure and intake. Soon you will be one of those enviable people who can eat to their heart's content without putting on weight. Regular exercise will help you regulate your cravings for sweets, and you will automatically prefer healthier foods. The side effect is wonderful: you shape and tone your body and build beautiful muscles - which in turn replace those unloved fat pads and also burn excess calories. At the same time, you develop better body awareness and get closer to your healthy ideal weight - in short, you feel good all over! Then it won't matter if you have a chocolate bar now and again.

A little motivational tip: sign up for a city run of your choice today. Five kilometres is doable even for the untrained (walk a lap if you have to) and you have a reason to start training right away.

10 Live mindfully

When you change your diet, look at your other habits too. What do you eat, why and how often? Do you like to go shopping when your wardrobe is full to bursting? Do you often seek distraction through the media, consumer goods and events? So don't just clean out your fridge, take the opportunity to look at your wardrobe, your diary or even your home. Be aware of your consumer behaviour and question it critically. When shopping, think about whether you really need the object of your desire - or what the real reason for the purchase is. Get to the bottom of the possible reason. Could it be dissatisfaction with your current life situation? A fight with your partner or girlfriend? Or simply boredom?

Practice mindfulness with the 'headline method': focus your thoughts on a specific activity in your daily life to which you give your full attention. Concentrate only on that, be in the here and now, and enjoy the moment.

The next time you have a craving for something sweet that you find hard to resist, give the piece of cake your full attention. Don't devour it, but take your time to enjoy it. Don't do anything else at the same time, ignore the phone and turn off the TV. If you consciously live in the here and now from now on, future cravings for sweets will become increasingly rare.

11 Breathe slim

Yoga is also a good way to combat sweet cravings. As we know, the breath plays an important role in the body-centred exercises of yoga. Pranayama means the control (yama) of life energy (prana) through breathing. Deep inhalation and exhalation stimulates the metabolism and oxygenates the cells. Breathing also has an important effect on blood circulation, the immune system and digestion. When we are stressed and hectic, we literally run out of breath. We usually breathe much too quickly and shallowly. As a result, oxygen does not fully reach the deeper internal organs in the abdomen, which is important for achieving relaxation and inner peace. We often don't even realise the holistic effect of breathing. Breathing is something we take for granted - and yet we cannot survive without it, even for a short time. When you have a sweet tooth, taking a deep breath is often enough to release the energy responsible for digestion and well-being. With the right conscious breathing technique, the craving for sweets disappears in a matter of seconds and we can literally breathe our way to slimness. The next time you are in a stressful situation, focus on your breathing instead of reaching for a bag of jelly babies. A little note on your computer screen saying 'Breathe in, breathe out' can help. Place your flat hand on your abdominal wall and make sure your breath reaches your lower abdomen. Sign up for a yoga class and learn special breathing techniques, postures and mindfulness exercises. Gyms, sports clubs and community centres usually offer good introductory programmes. You will see: Not only will you feel better and more relaxed in no time, your cravings for sweets will disappear too!

12 Laughing is the best cure

Laughing is good for you: it activates up to 80 different muscles. It strengthens the heart and immune system, lowers blood pressure and stimulates digestion. It releases a host of endorphins, which have a downright euphoric effect on the body, mind and soul. With healthy optimism, humour and serenity, you can laugh your sugar addiction away. The more joy and positive thoughts that fill you, the more this attitude becomes ingrained in your personality, which can even be demonstrated neuroscientifically in certain regions of the brain. That's why there are laughter yoga classes, laughter therapies and thousands of laughter clubs in over 60 countries. A day without laughter is a day wasted, Charlie Chaplin once said. Of course, no one can be in a good mood all the time. And laughter has to be learned. Just try to put aside negative thought patterns, perfectionism, unhealthy self-deprecation and an overzealous desire for approval and focus instead on the good things in life. You are in control of how your day turns out: Read a funny book, watch a comedy on TV, go to the cabaret, jot down funny stories in your notebook, watch children at play or let your partner tickle your funny bone. Don't take life so seriously and smile as often as you can - even in situations where it might seem inappropriate (traffic, jogging, stressful meetings). Because you know: humour is when you laugh anyway!

13 The miracle elixir of herbs

The medieval German mystic Hildegard von Bingen swore by the far-reaching healing powers of herbs, roots and leaves. Today, we can draw on these tried and tested medieval monastic recipes and harness the benefits of special herbal mixtures. There is, for example, the bitter star with its 18 different medicinal herbs: the alcoholic extract from the bitter plants not only stimulates the metabolism, but also curbs the craving for sweets enormously. However, be careful not to drink too much of it, as it has a very high alcohol content (up to 59 per cent). It should be diluted with water and drunk just before a meal.

An alternative is the wonder plant liquorice. As the name suggests, the dry, golden-brown leaves look a little like tree bark and have a sweet, spicy flavour. Liquorice is made from liquorice, among other things, but it is also used to treat hoarseness, coughs and stomach ailments.

The next time you have a sweet tooth, simply scald a few sticks of liquorice with hot water and drink it as tea or chew the rolled leaves (do not swallow) until the craving for sweets passes on its own. Medicinal herbs and liquorice are available over the counter from any pharmacy.

14 Spice up your life!

We often associate cinnamon with Christmas biscuits such as cinnamon stars, baked apple cake and cinnamon buns, or even mulled wine. Oriental cuisine uses what is probably the world's oldest spice in savoury dishes such as chicken drumsticks, potato dishes or spinach stew. Cinnamon is also a key ingredient in curry.

But the spice can do much more. Traditional Chinese medicine uses cinnamon as a cure-all for high blood pressure, bladder infections, pain and inflammation. And Hildegard von Bingen used the spice to bake the famous 'Nervenkuchen' (made from spelt flour, almonds, cinnamon, nutmeg and cloves). Cinnamon is a real sugar killer and therefore a fat burner! The spice regulates blood sugar levels, warms from the inside and helps with poor concentration. Add this special spice to your life outside the Christmas season: Try cinnamon in unsweetened fruit salad, cappuccino, hot chocolate or simply in milk. Freshly squeezed fruit juice, semolina porridge, muesli or unsweetened rice pudding will also take on a special flavour with this spice. Cinnamon is particularly good in tea: pour hot water over about three slices of ginger, cardamom, honey, a little milk and a pinch of cinnamon powder (or half a cinnamon stick). Wonderful!

15 Boost your immune system

A healthy lifestyle also has a positive effect on your immune system. By combining a healthy, sugar-free diet, exercise and rest (i.e. getting enough sleep and avoiding too much stress), your body will thank you by not jumping on the next flu wave. As an 'empty carbohydrate', sugar provides energy but contains no nutrients or vital substances. When you eat sugar, your gut flora is disrupted, your blood sugar levels spike and your immune system is weakened. Instead, choose foods that are rich in vitamins and vital substances to boost your immune system, such as broccoli, cabbage, carrots, spinach and lemons.

Ginger, tragacanth, ginseng or aloe vera roots can also help boost the immune system. Be physically active and cycle instead of taking the bus. This will reduce your exposure to airborne germs. Get moving and cycle instead of taking the bus. This will reduce your exposure to airborne germs.

And if you do get the flu, your body's defences will help you to recover more quickly. Don't automatically reach for painkillers, fever reducers or other medicines, some of which contain a lot of sugar. Allow your weakened body to respond naturally to the flu viruses, even if this means that the illness may last two to three days longer than with medication. Your immune system will emerge stronger overall. And remember, when you make a conscious decision to cut back on sugar in favour of healthy alternatives, you are also boosting your immune system!

16 Addiction & Desire

The terms and meanings of addiction and desire are very similar. The word search is also closely related. So the next time you have a craving for something sweet, ask yourself honestly what you are really looking for or craving. In most cases a craving for something sweet is a signal to look for the real cause. Is it something you like, something you crave and something you may not be able to get? Cravings always occur when something is missing. In a positive sense, it is part of us because it is the driving force that keeps us going until we find what we crave. It can be security, contentment, love, happiness, but it can also be fulfilment, recognition or direction. Go on a search and find out what your heart is really longing for. Often there are clearly identifiable problems and emotional deficits at the root of our longing, such as frustration with our partner, loneliness, stress at work or being overwhelmed by everyday tasks. They can usually be solved quite easily by making small changes (talking, more private meetings, delegating tasks, reducing working hours).

It becomes more difficult when wishes and desires seem unattainable. So don't set your personal goals too high. Write down your three biggest wishes and see if and how you can achieve them. Not everything has to be perfect, or the best, or the most expensive, or the biggest. While you are looking for the big fulfilment, you may miss the many small moments of happiness that are waiting for you if you are just open to them. Longing is a good thing, as long as it does not turn into addiction and dependence, compulsion or greed. Try to keep a balance here, otherwise change your perspective and enjoy the beautiful moments of everyday life!

17 Hypnosis can help

Hypnosis is becoming increasingly important in psychotherapy. Hypnosis is not hocus-pocus, but the achievement of a trance-like state through suggestion. Although the hypnotist has exceptional powers of observation and knowledge of human nature, and can usually interpret body language correctly, his hypnosis technique enables him to put the patient into a state of trance that leads to deep relaxation. Consciousness falls into a relaxed state and the patient appears to be absent (usually through simple distractions). With this method it is possible to gain access to the person's unconscious, to address it directly and to influence its information processing.

Hypnosis, in the form of autogenic training, hypnotherapy, positive thinking or meditation, is increasingly being used to induce deep relaxation and to break psychological dependencies such as addiction. These relaxation techniques can help to strengthen the psyche and direct thoughts to better achieve desired goals. Try them out: Which of the methods appeals to you the most? Which technique will help you achieve optimal deep relaxation? Try it out. You will see after a relatively short time: When you find yourself in a stressful situation, you will be able to deal with it much better and will no longer have to resort to the usual adrenaline rush.

Extra tip

Autogenic Training (AT) is easy to learn, can be done anytime, anywhere, and quickly helps you achieve greater calm and serenity. This relaxation technique based on autosuggestion is ideal for reducing cravings for sweets.

Take 3 to 30 minutes to find a quiet place where you can sit or lie down undisturbed and close your eyes. Begin by mentally repeating the formula 'calm, heaviness, warmth' several times, concentrating on your breathing, heartbeat and thoughts. Pay attention to your physical sensations and transfer the three positive words to your whole body. As with any exercise, repetition, practice and persistence are important.

Repeat the exercise until you feel completely relaxed. Autogenic training leads to greater serenity and awareness of your inner self. By using this relaxation technique, you can better identify the cause of your sweet cravings and simply train yourself.

Let go of old patterns

Congratulations, you are off and running! You are beginning to attract the attention of those around you with your dietary changes.

Admittedly, it's not always easy to follow your new path in everyday life. Wherever you look, sweet traps lurk. In the past, you would have succumbed to them quickly and without exception. Now you know the tricks! But beware: you may be able to decipher ingredient lists with ease, but you'll still be bombarded with curious questions about your new eating habits. But this shouldn't be a problem for you: In the following chapter, you will learn to break old habits, stand by your decisions, and not let other people's opinions influence you.

From now on, you will be able to take silly remarks or that tempting plate of cake on your desk in your stride. You may even find yourself surrounded by interested sugar addicts who want to share your new philosophy, and you may even become a role model.

Fighting the constant craving for sweets means, above all, lifelong learning. In this section, I will introduce you to important sources of motivation that can help you to free yourself from your sweet addiction for good: take inspiration from our ancestors, from the animal world, from Buddha and, of course, from love.

18 `Why don't you enjoy more!'

Isn't this saying getting on your nerves, don't you think? In this age of experience and affluence, it really has had its day. Giving up sweets is supposed to limit our lives, make everyday life more difficult and be hostile to pleasure? What nonsense! The food industry has already done a great job. In reality, it's the other way round: eating sweets all the time makes you tired, chubby, ill and moody. Where is the pleasure in that? It's not about going without, it's about making a conscious choice for a better, healthier, more vital life. Even sayings such as 'You used to love that too' or 'You've always had a sweet tooth, where did this change of heart come from? And if you have, you have all the more reason to change.

Think of it this way: you can change, think differently and gain new insights! And feel free to share your evolution with others. Their comments may have an envious undertone because they may not have their own sugar addiction under control. Don't be fobbed off with pet names such as 'sweet tooth' or 'junkie', which you never found particularly appropriate. From now on, you are the one who decides what characteristics are attributed to you.

My tip: Instead of sweets, treat yourself to something really good, such as a fruit cocktail, a spa day or just spending time with friends.

19 Are you a 'yes' person?

Already said no today? I hope so! You don't always have to conform for the sake of peace, compassion or duty. Say no to requests, offers or tasks at work, in your family or among friends if you can't say yes out of conviction. Consciously say no! We are constantly being wooed. Do you often find yourself trying to be all things to all people, to please everyone and offend no one? Then put aside your remorse and guilt and say no for once!

When you receive your next offer, enquiry or request, give yourself plenty of time to think about your decision. You don't have to decide right away. Don't be afraid of the consequences of refusing. Don't neglect your own needs. A no to others is often a yes to yourself! You will see that it will soon be much easier for you to resist the many advertising promises and bargain offers and to say no. Start with the first exercise: say no to tempting sweets. When you realise that you are doing something good for yourself, it will be easy to say no.

20 Really cool

Coolness plays a key role in our teenage years. But even beyond our twenties, a certain nonchalance and relaxed attitude looks good on us. A cool person is confident, calm and in control, and keeps a 'cool head' in the truest sense of the word, even in difficult situations. He or she is self-assured and has a sense of humour. You are already on the right track because giving up sugar impresses people and makes you really cool! When you feel good in your own skin, you automatically feel more confident.

It's like a chain reaction. Knowing you have beaten your sugar addiction gives you a sense of self-satisfaction, confidence and good cheer. And as the pounds fall off, you will soon have to clear out your wardrobe, which is a real reason to be happy. Your positive change will make those around you sit up and take notice. How is this possible, they will ask. Take more time for the finer things in life, because as cool as you are now, you are taking a more relaxed approach to everything.

Celebrate as much as you can: turn up the radio, sing or whistle along and shake your hips! And don't forget to wink at your reflection in the mirror. You should be proud of yourself!

21 Take action! Now!

Eating on the side has crept into our society: popcorn and ice cream at the cinema, snacks and finger food at parties, and cake with coffee in the afternoon. How can you reduce your sugar intake in the long term and avoid the constant temptation of sweets without becoming a party pooper? The most important thing is to never go to a party or get together with friends when you are hungry. That way, you won't be so quickly overcome by the desire for sweets. And if you do, you can curb your appetite by looking for healthy alternatives or by distracting yourself, for example by dancing or having a stimulating conversation with the nice man behind you in the buffet queue. Don't talk about food all the time, avoid rooms where food is the centre of attention and drink water if you feel the need to hold something in your hands.

And if the table at your company's annual Christmas party is laid as generously as ever, choose only the healthy snacks and don't eat out of boredom or solidarity. Such parties can sometimes be long and overflowing. Get some fresh air and exercise in between. Encourage your family and friends to get involved. Go for a walk together or organise a little race around the block. You will find that others will join in enthusiastically and suddenly you will be the 'feel-good hero'!

Extra tip

Bring your own snacks to the cinema, such as cashew nuts, dried tomatoes or handy fruit (apple slices, grapes). Hot tomato juice or sweet carrot juice are good drinks. They will fill you up and even improve your eyesight.

22 Your USP makes you interesting!

You step away from your desk for a moment and the plate with a tempting piece of cake is already on your table. Your colleague has been too good to you once again. What should you do? Say thank you for the kind gesture and try to get rid of the sweet piece as quickly as possible. You won't be doing anyone a favour if you politely eat it now and regret it later. Give it to a colleague who will appreciate it.

There are many occasions throughout the year when you will find yourself in this situation: birthdays, anniversaries, public holidays, graduations, farewells and, last but not least, everyday stressful times when your colleague tries to cheer you up with sweets. What do you do? It's up to you whether you accept out of courtesy, or politely decline.

Set an example, because there are other ways: next time you have the chance, bring a well-filled, colourful fruit basket to work or bake a delicious sugar-free bread with nuts, berries and cottage cheese. This will put you in a good mood, attract attention and fill you up. It will win you friends, earn you sympathy and gratitude - and create a unique selling point for your company.

USP (Unique Selling Proposition) is a marketing term for a unique selling proposition that guarantees success. If you ever fail or change jobs, people will be happy to remember your USP.

23 A green way to indulge

A long week at work has been filled with stress, hectic rushes and exhausting meetings. The last thing you want to do on your days off is go to the busy, noisy and crowded city centre to reward yourself with pointless shopping. What's more, you are constantly reminded to eat in the city centre. You work up an appetite even though your stomach is full (be aware of this).

My tip: opt for the tranquillity of nature and go for a long walk in the woods at the weekend for a change. Have you noticed the change of seasons this year? I don't mean the daily grumbling about the bad weather. Collect flowers, chestnuts, leaves and special stones or enjoy the picturesque sunset. Watch ducks diving or squirrels climbing. You'll see how little you crave sweets when you're out in nature. So visit your favourite green spaces as often as possible, maybe combine it with a daily jog around the lake. Or just enjoy an evening stroll in a beautiful park. Have little or no time? Combine your daily chores, commute or break with a short trip into the countryside. Where in your neighbourhood do you have quick access to nature? Does your commute take you past fields? Is the city park close to where you work? Or is it the wood behind your house or the river in the centre of town? Look for green oases where you can recharge your batteries.

24 The freedom trap

If you take a closer look at human history, you will be amazed at how free we are to live our lives today - unlike our ancestors. In the Western world at least, we are largely free to choose where we live, where we work and who we marry. We can choose our religion, our hobbies and how we spend our money.

What a luxury! We should be in a constant state of happiness - instead, mental and physical suffering dominates the human condition. Why is this so? What are we missing? Why are we sometimes so unhappy, dissatisfied, stressed and ill?

There are two sides to every coin: the variety of options not only gives us more freedom. We are also spoilt for choice. Traditional family structures are breaking down as a result of increasing individualisation; we are becoming loners and workaholics. Suddenly we have problems of orientation because we can no longer hold on to old values. It's no wonder that we sometimes fall for the attractive promises of the advertising industry. It creates its products according to our wishes and desires, it creates images with which we identify only too readily, it butter us up and, thanks to skilful product staging, we are suddenly overcome by an insatiable desire for sweets.

Every advert can be a sugar trap for us. Take the test and turn on the TV. Scrutinise every advert and uncover the messages behind them. If you scrutinise and consistently reduce your media consumption, instead spending more time in the fresh air and much more time offline, the deceptive sweet cravings will surely be silenced.

25 Strong together

Are you a sugar addict again? You are not alone! Find allies, companions and like-minded people to talk to. Encourage each other and pluck yourself up in times of weakness. Confide in your closest friends, family and work colleagues. Explain your new eating habits or lifestyle change to them; this is the only way you will be understood and supported. Then no one will blame you for refusing sweets. Setbacks, which are bound to happen from time to time, are easier to deal with if you have someone to talk to. And you're not alone.

Extra tip

Interessante Webseiten zu alternativen Ernährungs- und Lebensweisen sind zum Beispiel:

- https://www.drlibby.com
- https://daniellewalker.com oder
- https://www.mysugarfreekitchen.com
- https://www.spoonfulofsugarfree.com
- https://baketotheroots.de

If you don't meet like-minded people from the start, within a few weeks you will have a few interested people around you. You will be amazed at how much there is to talk about and how many people want to reduce their sugar intake. You will always have something to talk about in the company canteen and, if necessary, at boring dinner parties. You can share recipes, methods and experiences, as well as laugh about setbacks, everyday pitfalls or failures. Search the internet for groups, forums and blogs. You are sure to meet like-minded people, as well as exotic people who may contribute completely different ideas. And who knows, you might even find some of the ideas of the neo-minimalists, the sharing community, the organic gurus, the raw foodists or the paleo-followers interesting.

Sugar-free recipe ideas on the following pages: Healthy snacking can be so easy. All the products featured here are homemade and guaranteed to contain no (industrial) sugar. Alternatives include xylitol, stevia or pureed/chopped dates.

26 The way through the heart is (not only) through its stomach

All you need is love! Emotional chaos, heart palpitations and butterflies in your stomach are the signs of true infatuation. Love also makes the feeling of hunger disappear. Living on air and love" - many newly in love couples know this. Your hormones are going crazy, you can't think of anything else, and you can barely get a bite to eat. No wonder the pounds are falling off. And while your emotions are on a rollercoaster, you're literally in seventh heaven.

From a biological point of view it is understandable that this state does not last forever. The initial euphoria (triggered by dopamine) is followed by excitement (triggered by adrenaline) and finally a rush of happiness and a deep sense of well-being (triggered by endorphins and cortisol). Love, contentment and happiness are therefore closely linked. However, the emotional rush subsides once our hormone levels have calmed down. No matter - just keep going and keep rekindling those feelings!

How do you do this? For example, by giving compliments more often, giving flowers and hugging your loved ones. Have you done anything loving today? Any form of love - be it self-love, compassion or an intimate partnership - can trigger such a feeling of elation. So as you sink into the flow of love, have intense encounters with friends or lend a helping hand to desperate work colleagues, you forget your everyday worries and problems, including your pesky appetite for sweets. In this state, you live in the here and now, you relax the best and you have the most creative ideas. Take advantage of the endless possibilities of love and let it inspire you!

27 Thanks to Buddha

You might think that when Buddha formulated the so-called 'Four Noble Truths' as a path to enlightenment some 2,500 years ago, he would have had an inkling of our sugar problem. He blamed three traits for our daily suffering: greed, anger and ignorance. All three 'basic evils' are interrelated and can be applied to almost all areas of life. Greed refers to avarice as well as lust, addiction or the desire to have. When greed is not satisfied, it often develops into anger, pessimism or rage. Ignorance is synonymous with delusion or ignorance.

This sounds very familiar: Your thoughts constantly revolve around that sweet piece of chocolate (greed). Once you've finished the bar, you feel guilty and angry at yourself and your weak willpower (anger). All because we didn't realise where the greed and loss of control came from (ignorance). In short, Buddha's antidote is this: Letting go. The best way to do this is with mindfulness. You can consciously counteract the three harmful qualities and their chain reaction by acquiring the appropriate knowledge, organising your daily life mindfully and remaining calm.

Remember Buddha's words the next time you have a craving for sugar. By acquiring knowledge, you have already overcome your 'delusion', your ignorance in this matter. You alone determine your thoughts, distract them with beautiful things, for example, and pay no further attention to greed. With this mindful attitude, the craving for sweets will soon disappear and nothing will stand in the way of your 'enlightenment'.

28 Our true home

Many people take great pride in having a beautiful home. They invest a lot of time and money in making it perfect. Weekends and holidays are spent in DIY stores and furniture stores to decorate and improve the home. New trends, changes, but also cracks in the wall.

What most people forget, however, is that our true home is ourselves. Our body is our temple. It is where we live until the end of our days. In order to feel comfortable in our own skin, we need to take care of it, shape it and give it the attention it deserves. Yet many people neglect their bodies almost criminally. They don't have the time and would rather tend to the garden or redecorate than shed those extra pounds. So consciously turn your attention back to your real home! Take care of yourself by caring for your body and reducing your sugar intake. Be grateful for your health, appearance and physical abilities (which we often take for granted). Do a 'body scan' in the form of a meditation or conscious mindfulness exercise and focus your attention on your body. Choose a comfortable position and make sure you can do the exercise in peace. Be aware of your thoughts, sensations and feelings. Focus your attention on your breathing and different parts of your body. Feel your body in your mind, from your feet to the tip of your nose.

You will learn to consciously listen to your inner voice again. Of course, you need to sweat a little. Why not combine your workout with some housework: digging in the garden, cycling to the bakery or chopping wood yourself. By cutting out sweets, you are also doing yourself a favour by delaying your body's next 'renovation'. So you can sit back in your cosy furniture lounge and enjoy your beautiful home.

29 Learning from history

Why do people study things that are long gone? All over the world there are studies, documentaries and institutions that deal with the past. But why? Surely we should be concentrating on the present and preparing for the future? Or should we? For one simple reason: we want to learn from mistakes and experiences. The past is the source of all our knowledge today, it is what we orient ourselves to, it is what our whole world is based on, and so it is worth looking at past eras.

Let's go back to the Stone Age. How did our ancestors eat? How and why has our diet changed since then? n the Neolithic period, the so-called New Stone Age (around 10,000 years ago), humans underwent a major upheaval that still shapes our diet today. With the onset of sedentarisation, or the establishment of settlements, our ancestors developed agriculture and animal husbandry, which significantly changed the original hunter-gatherer diet. Cereals such as emmer, einkorn, naked wheat and barley began to be eaten. But cheesecake, fruit yoghurt and white bread rolls would not have been on our ancestors' menus. So we should opt for the original, fresh and natural foods. The Stone Age is still in our bones.

Now there are many revivals, such as the Paleo movement, which is based on Stone Age diets and incorporates prehistoric conditions into modern life: From exercising more to cutting out sugar to walking barefoot. Try the Paleo lifestyle for a day. You don't have to wrap yourself in furs or build fires. How about a wheat-free week or minimalist shoes? And definitely try to avoid industrial sugar. After all, it is a relatively recent development.

30 Learning from animals

Do you have pets? Then you know we can learn a lot about nutrition and happiness from them, whether they are dogs, cats, hamsters or guinea pigs. Animals are usually alert, curious and playful or, when they have eaten, full and satisfied. Animals only eat when they are hungry and can stop eating when they are full. However, we are seeing more and more cats and dogs becoming overweight, suffering from allergies, diabetes or even tooth decay. Maybe it's the canned food (usually loaded with additives and sugar), maybe it's the lack of exercise, or maybe it's both.

But in nature, animals are true models of nutrition: they spend all day looking for food. For them, hunting or gathering, eating and resting are in a balanced relationship. This reminds us of our ancestors, like Kennewick Man. Not so long ago, humans were constantly on the move in search of natural food sources, adapting to their environment for survival. It was only when we became sedentary and food became more readily available that this original way of life changed. However, our animal relatives still have an instinct that tells them when they have eaten enough. We should take a leaf out of their book and pay more attention to our natural sense of satiety. With or without children, visit the zoo and be inspired! Go on a voyage of discovery and watch the lions eat. It goes without saying that you should give the ice-cream vendor a wide berth this time.

31 Even children learn it (wrongly)

'I want that!' The little ones are already pointing at the brightly colored packaging in the supermarket—placed conveniently at their eye level, of course. With cute characters, eye-catching designs, and sugary flavors, these products—referred to in German as Quängelware ("pester power goods")—are specifically crafted to target children's emotions. Unfortunately, many of these items are unhealthy due to their high sugar content. But your child doesn't care about that; they just want the colorful bag of candy. To protect your child, try simple strategies, like positioning the stroller so they can see you instead of the entire store. Limit their exposure to stimuli as much as possible. At home, reduce their screen time, as TV advertising constantly pushes these products. Instead, use your shared time for exciting activities, games, or reading aloud together.

As parents, we are role models for our children. Kids imitate everything we do, shaping their actions and thoughts based on our behavior. This becomes especially tricky when it comes to sweets. If we indulge in frequent snacking, it's hard to deny sweets to our kids. If we forbid them entirely, they may perceive sugary treats as both forbidden and desirable, making them even more appealing. Instead, teach your child early on about the effects of industrial sugar on the body and model healthy eating habits yourself. After all, what applies to children applies to adults as well!

By taking responsibility for ourselves and our choices, we can also set a positive example for our society. Without being dogmatic, we can share our knowledge of healthy eating with others and encourage a more balanced approach to food.

Ready for new strategies

Want to keep going in the future? Then get inspired by these tips with real long-term benefits.

Keep an eye on your sugar addiction by developing strategies to add structure and control to your sugar-free routine. This will help you consolidate your successes in the long term. For example, regular diary entries, a new weekly plan or learning more about healthy eating can help.

And don't forget to reward yourself for giving up sugar - it's a great way to stay motivated! There are no limits to your creativity. If you're in a good mood and thinking positively, you won't feel like eating sweets in the first place: find out which power fruits can lift your spirits, why sour lemons make you happy and why a sugar-free diet is the best beauty tip.

What has giving up sweets got to do with your health? As you already know, a lot: whether you want to boost your immune system, stay fit for longer or simply give your body and mind a break during Lent, there are so many ways to do something good for yourself by changing your diet.

Your next holiday can also be a real challenge - sugar free - by discovering new foods and dishes to enrich your diet. And if you're not planning a trip to faraway lands this year, why not take a culinary trip to other countries and try new recipes you've never tried before - the new taste experiences will soon make you forget your sweet tooth.

To put a permanent end to your sugar addiction, try to free yourself from your destructive thought patterns and practise patience. After all, practice makes perfect, so what's the rush?

32 The no-sugar diary

Similar to visualization (discussed in another chapter of this book), keeping a no-sugar diary can be a powerful tool to help you succeed. Here's how to get started: Take your regular diary and mark the successful days with a symbol, such as a "Z" for zero sugar. Celebrate as these marks begin to accumulate! Before long, you might find yourself flipping the system—marking only the days when the "sugar bug" bites.

For an even better overview, consider using an annual calendar that you can stick on your fridge. Add other symbols, like "S" for sport, "M" for meditation, or "Y" for yoga. Reward yourself with a big smiley for a successful week—it's a fun way to stay motivated!

The goal of the diary is to help you visualize and track your sugar habits. Most importantly, it gives you a no-sugar plan. Write down exactly when and why you reached for something sweet. Be honest with yourself—note every detail.

For example, your log might look like this:

- *Monday, 10 a.m.: Stress at the office, mountain of paperwork → Ate a chocolate bar (approx. 20 g).*

- *3 p.m.: Afternoon slump, cravings after a heavy canteen lunch, bad mood, rainy weather → Ate 3 cookies (60 g) with a cup of hot chocolate (250 ml).*

It all adds up, doesn't it? By using this method, you'll quickly identify your triggers and habits. With this book as your guide, you'll soon be on the path to breaking free from sugar addiction.

33 Downshifting with a simple rule

Is your working day characterised by daily deadline pressure, stress and hectic pace? Add to that long commutes, short breaks and endless to-do lists? Then there are good reasons for your unhealthy eating habits - the temptation to make a pilgrimage to the confectionery aisle or the local bakery is just too great in times of stress. You know it, but you don't have the courage to deal with it.

What helps? Structure your life according to a rule called the 'A-B-C rule': First the necessary (A), then the possible (B), and finally the impossible (C). So you don't have to work half days or go to the gym. Even if you work a ten-hour day, you can make a conscious effort to slow down and do something for your health: Incorporate as much movement as possible into your daily routine (A), for example by doing short yoga exercises as soon as you get up: Sun Salutation in the bedroom and Warrior Pose while brushing your teeth. Cycle or walk to work and so on. Focus on one thing at a time during the day. Take proper (lunch) breaks and, if possible, do not answer the phone during these times. Get out of the office and find a quiet place to rest. Choose healthy, unsweetened snacks such as apples, nuts or cherry tomatoes, and always take your water bottle with you.

You have already achieved a lot for half the day: you have eaten well, exercised and even managed to relax a little.

Do the rest of your tasks in the second half of the day (B) and look forward to the end of the day. Also, learn to leave things lying around that you didn't get done during the day. The more free time you have, the more productive you will be.

As long as you stick to the A-B sequence, you will automatically get things done that you thought were impossible (C). If you follow this simple A-B-C rule in the future, you can look forward to an increase in your wellbeing!

Extra tip

In addition to the piece of fruit or nut packet, the outdoor travel cutlery 'Foon' (fork and spoon combined) for spontaneous salads or yoghurts always belongs in your hand luggage, as well as a food storage container as a plate replacement for quick muesli mixes and a leak-proof thermos flask for homemade cocoa in between - sugar-free, of course.

34 The no-sugar masterplan

The longer you study sugar addiction, the deeper you will delve into the subject. Whole new and exciting topics will open up - suddenly you'll be looking at human history, sustainability, shopping addiction and alcohol consumption. You might even buy a specialist book or read scientific articles on nutrition. In this way, you will gradually acquire a broad knowledge of eating behaviour, evolutionary biology and addiction research, and discover exciting approaches from anthropology, neurology and ancient Greece.

Explore the history of human nutrition or be inspired by the archaeological finds of the last Stone Age skeletons at the Ethnological Museum. Of course, it could also take you in a completely different direction. No matter where your curiosity takes you, you will gain exciting new knowledge that will be an interesting topic of conversation at the next party. When the subject of sugar comes up, you are sure to shine with facts and historical background. And the more you know, the less likely you are to fall into the sugar trap. Become a sugar-free nutrition expert and banish sugar addiction from your life forever. What topic are you most interested in and where would you like to learn more?

35 Pure creativity

Whether you're shopping at the supermarket or cooking at home, you'll learn to reorganise your everyday life. Cutting out sugar encourages creativity! The more imaginative you are when baking and cooking, the more fun you will have. So don't get upset about the difficulties in everyday life that cutting out sugar may cause, such as not having everything readily available and easy to buy. Look at the perceived problem with calm and composure.

Become Alice in Wonderland and turn your surroundings into an enchanted forest: turn physalis into sweets, curd cheese with fresh fruit into a new delicious ice cream flavour. Bake cookies with bananas or cherries and give them funny names.

For example, when I make my hazelnut, coconut and date biscuits, they make a funny clapping noise, so my friends call them 'clapping biscuits'. My chocolate cake, made with almond flour, cocoa, walnuts, fresh raspberries and bananas, is called 'Fitti cake' because it gives you a lot of energy and is particularly good as a snack during sports activities. What are the names of your new creations? High time for a recipe book, don't you think?

36 Sour makes one funny

The original German saying goes, "sour stimulates the appetite." This proverb has been common in German-speaking countries since the 17th century. Does a similar expression exist in your language? In any case, there's some truth to it: sour really does awaken the appetite. It stimulates the taste buds, invigorates the senses, and makes eating more enjoyable—adding a touch of fun to the experience.

Just think of a lemon. The moment you picture it, your eyes automatically narrow, the corners of your mouth turn up, and a smile spreads across your face. There's even solid neurological evidence to back up the mood-lifting effects of sour foods. They trigger the production of serotonin, a neurotransmitter that boosts your mood and sharpens your focus.

Among the top ten sour favorites are pickles, sour herring, lemons, green apples, sauerkraut, rhubarb, sour cherries, redcurrants, sea buckthorn, and sour milk. Besides their tangy taste, acidic foods are packed with vitamin C and essential minerals. Fermented sour milk products, for example, are rich in lactic acid bacteria. These bacteria are crucial for strengthening the immune system, eliminating harmful bacteria, and maintaining the body's acid-base balance. Sour foods don't just affect humans—they intrigue animals too! Watching a dog accidentally bite into a lemon instead of a tennis ball, for instance, is bound to make you laugh. So, what are your favorite sour foods? Add them to your shopping list and enjoy their benefits from now on!

37 Great little power fruits

The world's largest river, the Amazon in South America, with its vast quantities of water, produces many a miracle plant in the tropical rainforest. The cacao tree and the guarana bush are among these power plants. Although we may think of sweet milk chocolate or powdered milk drinks, cocoa is much more than that!

Extra tip

Recipe for Herb Power Bread (gluten-free and guaranteed sugar-free!):

- 200g ground almonds
- 2 tbsp grated coconut
- 2 tbsp flaxseed (crushed)
- 2 tbsp freshly chopped herbs (of your choice)
- 5 eggs
- 1 sachet baking powder
- 30ml melted coconut oil
- 1 pinch of salt
- 1 tbsp apple cider vinegar

Put the almonds, coconut flour, linseed flour and herbs in a bowl and mix with the eggs, oil and vinegar until you have a thick mixture. Add the salt and baking powder and heat the oven to 200°C. Pour the mixture into a greased loaf tin. Bake for about 1/2 hour at 180°C until the crust is golden brown and firm. Check the consistency with a toothpick: if nothing sticks, your Herb Power Bread is ready to eat.

The Aztecs considered cocoa to be the fruit of the gods. Cocoa was said to have healing powers. No wonder, as the bean is extremely healthy and rich in vitamins. The great thing is that today we can buy pure cocoa powder without sugar or other additives in any major supermarket.

Look in the bakery section where you will usually find cocoa next to nuts, icing and flour. Pour the powder into a glass (one to two teaspoons) and add a little hot water to dissolve it before adding the milk. Try the powder with soy, almond or rice milk and perhaps a pinch of cinnamon. You will be amazed at how good these cocoa drinks taste without sugar. Delicious!

The caffeinated guarana plant is equally nutritious and stimulating. The powder, which is made from the ground seeds of the guarana fruit, can be bought in shops around the world or online. Guarana is often used in this country as a healthy alternative to coffee beans and is often used in sports. The powder is usually taken dissolved in water. It curbs the appetite (especially for sweets), stimulates the circulation and lifts the mood. Aren't these great fruits?

38 Living like God in France

Interestingly, the phrase "live like God in France" became a popular saying after the French Revolution at the end of the 18th century. Not only was the Catholic Church overthrown in France, but God himself was replaced by reason. Since then, the expression "live like God in France" has become widely used across Europe, with slight variations such as "eat like God in France" in German.

French cuisine is regarded as the pinnacle of culinary art in Europe. France is famous for its exceptional wines and delicious cheeses. In addition to iconic dishes like baguettes, crêpes, tarte flambée, and quiche, the menu features a variety of fish, lamb, seafood, vegetables, and fresh herbs. There are also exquisite dishes made with aubergines, mussels, and duck. In France, eating is an experience focused on savoring every bite—and the French certainly set a great example.

Why not enrich your recipe collection with delightful, naturally sugar-free dishes from French cuisine? Our taste buds deserve some variety! Take the artichoke, for example. Both the leaves and the base of the flower are edible. You can boil, fry, or grill this vibrant green vegetable. Artichoke hearts are particularly delicious when pickled as an antipasto. For a treat, try artichokes baked with cheese on slices of baguette or toss them into a fresh salad. Bon appétit!

39 Kitchen cosmetics

Wouldn't it be great if you never had to spend money on expensive hair treatments, nail polish for brittle fingernails or lotions for blemished skin? The good news is that by avoiding industrial sugar, you can actually improve the appearance of your skin within days, your fingernails within weeks and your hair within days. And all of this can be achieved with a simple change in your diet: put more emphasis on a healthy and balanced diet. Eat lots of fresh fruit and whole grains instead of sweets. Eat more nuts and linseeds (they are particularly rich in zinc, vitamins and minerals) and you will soon not only feel better, but look healthier too.

You can also help from the outside: Face masks, creams and oils with ingredients from the garden. As the saying goes, only use products you would eat. After work, indulge in a little pampering: treat your dark circles with cucumber slices, soak your feet in an aromatic herbal bath or massage the ends of your hair with olive oil or aloe vera. You will feel wonderfully refreshed and rejuvenated.

40 The best pension plan

When it comes to our pensions, we are probably the best pension experts around. We invest our money, take out insurances and additional financing in good time. We leave nothing to chance when it comes to our future, don't we?

But when it comes to eating, we are often far too careless, sometimes even negligent. Too often, due to lack of time, convenience or ignorance, we choose unhealthy foods that can even harm us. Yet our health depends so much on what we eat!

We have known for a long time that a balanced, healthy diet has a positive effect on the body and mind. So how about a real prevention plan for a healthy retirement? For a good start to the day, we recommend a rich breakfast with high-quality proteins, fats and carbohydrates. How about a healthy, crunchy muesli? Cut fruit into bite-sized pieces for the office - in case you fancy something sweet later on. Take at least an hour for lunch and try to cover everything your body needs for the rest of the day: some carbohydrates (potatoes or vegetables), enough protein and fat (from flaxseed, eggs or fish). For dessert, combine fruit of your choice with yoghurt or cottage cheese. Nuts, almonds or dried fruit are good snacks. Drink at least one and a half litres of fluid throughout the day - not including the four cups of coffee in the morning! Look forward to your well-earned dinner, which should not be too late (four hours before bedtime is ideal). How about a fresh salad, some grilled chicken, a homemade soup or simply a sugar-free protein shake? At the end of the day, treat yourself to a cup of unsweetened tea of your choice and settle down in time for a good night's sleep - and you'll be set for old age!

41 Take a healthy break

The year has barely begun when many people begin the traditional Lenten fast on Ash Wednesday, six weeks before Easter. The Christian cleansing ritual is meant to remind us of Jesus' 40-day fast in the desert. Today, fasting is no longer automatically associated with religion. The focus can be on consciously detoxifying one's body or the need to take time out to rid oneself of superfluous baggage and get rid of old, unpleasant habits.

Fasting has a positive effect on the body, mind and soul: The release of endorphins brings inner harmony, happiness, peace and lightness. Sensory impressions are more intense and you take time to review old habits. Fasting can also be combined with more exercise (e.g. yoga), relaxation (plenty of sleep) and conscious body care (including a healthy diet). There are many different types of fasting: alkaline fasting, for example, allows you to eat small meals throughout the day. These should be alkaline and rich in minerals to deacidify the body. Avoid sweets in particular, but also meat and dairy products, fish, pasta, coffee and alcohol.

Eat plenty of fruit and vegetables, and drink plenty of unsweetened tea or water, perhaps with a slice of lemon or a mint leaf to refresh. Above all, Lent is a great time to break the sugar habit and adopt new healthy habits. So why not use the traditional Lent of spring as your own personal healthy break? You don't have to do the whole

40 days. Just a few days are enough to make a real difference.

42 Treat yourself!

Of course, giving up sweets can also save you a lot of money. Let's do a quick calculation: You buy an average of one sweet a day, usually in the morning on your way to work at the bakery (about $2). In between, you reach into the drawer and buy a bar of chocolate or candy (about $3). After lunch, you have a coke or a small dessert ($3). In the evening, they have jelly beans or cookies with the TV on, or an ice cream ($2). Some people eat twice as much, others only at the weekend, but on average we spend maybe $10 a day on sweets and sugary products. That's $300 a month and $15,600 a year (you have to think about it, it's crazy!).

This convinces you to finally take action: create a small piggy bank and put in the dollars you would have spent on a chocolate bar at the supermarket checkout or on sweets at the bakery. Even avoiding energy drinks, sweetened fruit yoghurts or sandwiches will save you money. By the end of the year, you will have saved a tidy sum and cut out unnecessary calories. Congratulations! Now you can buy yourself something really special with your savings. Reward yourself with an extra holiday, for example. You'll probably need to do some shopping first, because you've probably lost a few kilos by cutting out sweets and you're in desperate need of a new bikini or swimsuit...

43 Set clear goals

There are people who really need to be precise. If you are also a perfectionist and an analytical person, make a strategic plan to get your sweet tooth under control. When exactly do you want to achieve what? What are the steps along the way? How will you go about it, what will you cut out of your diet, how much exercise will you do each week and what should the end result be? Think one step further: who will help you achieve your goals and who will stand in your way? Think about which roads you want to avoid and what you no longer want to do. Studies show that visualising goals creates a helpful structure to make the project more successful.

There are a number of techniques that can help: a 'mind map', a memory map with lots of graphic symbols, arrows and colours, or a list with a chronological list and bullet points. Keep it simple and use only one page to plan your sugar-free day. If you enter your plan as a list on your PC, you can add to it later.

For example, make a daily or weekly plan. Write down your milestones, cooking ideas or new habits. Remind yourself visually of your plans and reward yourself for achieving small goals. Because of the complexity of our daily lives, we constantly need to organise, structure and simplify our lives. Use symbols related to health (apple), exercise (wheel), well-being (smiley face) or happiness (clover leaf). Always carry the plan with you: take a photo of it with your smartphone or use it as a wallpaper on your device. However, refrain from giving specific weights. Instead of working towards a specific target weight, focus on your personal wellbeing. No one will notice if you weigh three kilos more or less, but they will notice your positive attitude. Don't be too hard on yourself and don't put yourself under unnecessary pressure. Just listen to your common sense.

44 The three-day rule

You've worked hard, fasted all day and still can't see any difference on the scales? Does this sound familiar? We all want to see instant results! But here's the key: be patient and give your body time to adjust. There's something called the 'three-day rule'. Have you heard of it? It's simple: the results of a plan or action won't be noticeable for three days - but I promise they will come! Try this challenge: Exercise for one hour every day for three consecutive days and give up sweets completely. You will see and feel the difference!

Of course, the three-day rule also works the other way round (and that's the tricky bit). If you treat yourself to a large piece of cake today and then snack on a bag of jelly babies later, you may get a stomach ache, but you won't suddenly gain three kilos. And why is that? Because digestion takes up to 72 hours. It takes three full days for the effects to become noticeable, for example when you realise that you can no longer fasten the button on your jeans. By then, the cake you ate three days ago is long forgotten and the context is often lost. You can no longer explain the 'mysterious' weight gain.

So stay away from sugary and fattening foods, lace up your trainers and go for a run instead. Practise the art of patience - because as the saying goes: 'Patience in all things leads to success!'

45 Nature sweets

Sometimes the craving for sweets is so overwhelming that you can hardly control it. Then bite into a crunchy apple, eat a banana or drink a big glass of water. Sometimes we confuse thirst with hunger, or even with feeling cold or tired. The first thing to do is find out what is causing your craving. If it is low blood sugar, try a natural alternative: dried fruit. Although they have a high natural sugar content (up to 55 per cent), they also contain valuable nutrients. Dates are a real source of energy and their high fibre content helps with digestion. They also contain a lot of magnesium, iron and vitamins B and C. They are popular as a snack, as a side dish in Mediterranean cuisine, or even as a main ingredient in pasta or meat dishes. Ripened in the Mediterranean sun, the fruit goes well with many other dishes: Yoghurt, cottage cheese, nuts, oranges, but also bacon, cheese or couscous.

Extra tip

Dried fruit alternatives without added (industrial) sugar are dates, figs, sultanas, grapes, peach, papaya, rhubarb or pineapple pieces, apple rings, banana pieces, pears, physalis, blueberries, apricots, plums, goji berries and mulberries. Be careful with cranberries, cherries, pieces of ginger, strawberries, kiwi, banana chips or mango: they are often sweetened!

So next time you fancy something sweet with your afternoon coffee, try some sweet dried fruit. It's best to portion them out first, as there's a big risk of eating more than you need. Three a day is no problem! If you don't like nuts and dried fruit, dark chocolate is a good dessert. The higher the cocoa content, the lower the sugar content. Have you ever tried 99% cocoa?

Another tip: never store sweets in any form at home or in your desk drawer! Trick your sugar addiction and make sure you have to reach for extra sweets when you have a craving. The strong craving will often go away on its own. And if you do take a few steps and the craving is still there, then you deserve a little snack!

46 Avoid negations

When formulating your goals, avoid using negative phrases such as 'you must not' or 'this is not allowed'. Such rules and restrictions tend to be demotivating and we don't like that. Life is hard enough as it is, we don't want to be forbidden to snack. Overcoming our sugar addiction should be a positive challenge and, above all, fun! Approach it with conviction, curiosity, openness and joy and you will find that you will soon be happy to give up too much sugar all by yourself! So don't make it too hard on yourself, and set yourself a relaxed no-sugar plan.

Write three positive sentences every day and use only positive words. Don't be afraid to create words like happy time, happiness formula, super project, power meal, best way, pig dog winner, master plan, etc. Don't forget the emoticons and take a break in between. Instead of saying 'I have to run six more miles today', say something positive: I can (or may) go for a leisurely jog. Turn the prohibition 'I can't eat chocolate' into a joyful expectation: 'I'm going to treat myself to a freshly squeezed pink grapefruit juice today. I will never manage to lose three kilos' becomes 'Today I feel good, no matter what the scales say'.

Speaking of scales: banish such mood killers from your field of vision - you'll be amazed at the positive effect this has on your weight!

47 Look forward

If you know the following saying, it may help you to remember it: 'A few seconds on the tongue, a few hours in the stomach, but years on the hips'. o every time you buy a new bar of chocolate, think about whether you really want to have a long-term relationship with your love handles. Be proactive and keep reminding yourself of this principle (with a reminder on your kitchen cupboard or a cheat sheet in your wallet). This little treat is short-lived. And because it is so fleeting, you are likely to repeat it all the more often. And you're already in the snack trap.

But instead of fighting cravings, make peace with your guilty conscience and take your time. Of course, you can still enjoy sweet treats! Snacking should be pleasurable, but make a conscious choice to enjoy smaller portions that you'll savor even more. Don't snack constantly—allow longer breaks between meals and listen to your body's natural signals of fullness. Avoid not only sugary foods but also those that are overly salty or fatty, as they'll only leave you craving more.

Stay positive! You can look forward to healthy, balanced, and delicious meals that leave you feeling satisfied without the bloated, overstuffed feeling.

Drinking plenty of fluids between meals (water, tea, less juice and coffee) will almost automatically regulate your appetite. Make sure you have the right products on your kitchen shelves and plenty of teas and bottled water. And remember to get some fresh air every day!

48 Explore

And what about holidays? You're right: you can get pretty comfortable on holiday. And that's a good thing - you want to relax and have fun. Food is often prepared and served by other people's hands.

Extra tip

Plan B for immediate use in the event of a sugar craving when you find it difficult to act with foresight:

- Briefly close your eyes and take a deep breath
- Drink a glass of mineral water
- Eat a piece of fruit
- Leave the room or get some fresh air.
- Do push-ups, sit-ups or strength exercises with dumbbells.
- Do breathing exercises on your back and rub your stomach with warm hands
- Go for a short jog
- Take your mind off things by listening to upbeat music and singing or dancing along.
- Call your best friend
- Jump in the shower
- Put on warmer clothes

Naturally, this luxury tempts you to eat large portions. That's why you should always ask yourself whether you really need to put all that food in your stomach. You don't have to throw all your good intentions overboard just because you're on holiday and the trip may have been very expensive. If you find this difficult, how about half board next time? Or go foraging in your holiday destination (if you can). Not only is it fun, but it also encourages exploration.

A holiday could also be a good opportunity to awaken your 'Stone Age instincts' (see previous tip in this book). You can discover culinary diversity in foreign countries. Keep two things in mind: enjoy naturally and in moderation. Take your time and observe how the locals eat. Be inspired and discover the country with all your senses.

49 Never give up!

'Don't give up` is the motto if you want to get your unhealthy snacking habits under control. There will certainly be days when you fall off the wagon, when you feel dissatisfied or weak. But every day is a new day to focus on your goals and good intentions and give up industrial sugar.

A little help is to set a day/date and focus on it: On day X I will officially give up sugar. How nice it would be to celebrate every week without sugar. And if it turns into months or even years, what an achievement! Make this day your own personal holiday. Invite friends and family over for a meal, serve sugar-free alternatives, show them what you can eat and enjoy without sugar! You'll see: A lot will come together and the table will be bountiful. Look back on the past year, with all its ups and downs. You weren't always steadfast? Never mind. Surely there were plenty of days when you persevered bravely and felt a real sense of achievement.

Celebrate your strength! How did you manage to stay off sugar for those days? What trick did you use and how did it make you feel? Be patient and understanding with yourself.

Laugh about your old 'addictive behaviour' today and be happy that you made such an important decision for yourself on day X. Perhaps today is such a day with the purchase of this guide?

If so, write the date on the next line:

____

So that you feel great about your achievements and don't miss out on the fun, try to find a natural balance between steadfastness, guilt and exceptions. You'll find it's not so hard!

50 Practice makes the pro

The well-known German saying "Übung macht den Meister" (practice makes perfect) is preceded by the phrase "Lehre bildet den Geist" (teaching strengthens the mind). Up until now, you've read a lot of valuable information. Maybe you've already put some of these tips into action and feel like you've got your sugar cravings under control—congratulations! But remember, no one becomes a master overnight. It's through repetition that new habits stick. You'd be surprised at how quickly we forget new information, and before you know it, you might fall back into old patterns. Thankfully, you've written everything down, so you always have a reminder handy.

Take time to review the chapters of this guide. Stay alert and mentally prepared for everyday challenges—the next birthday party is just around the corner, the holidays will arrive soon, and those tempting chocolate bars are always waiting at the checkout line. But if you stay calm and take a lighthearted approach, these sweet temptations won't throw you off course. The sugar traps are predictable—they appear every day. Pay attention to what works for you and what doesn't, and adjust your strategies as needed. Believe in yourself, and keep moving forward! I wish you all the best on your sugar-free journey!

Self-test: Are you addicted to sugar?

Not everyone who enjoys the occasional piece of cake or ice cream is immediately addicted to sweets. The transition from an occasional sweet tooth to a 'sugar junkie' is fluid. This test can help you find out where you currently stand.

Answer the following questions honestly to find out if you are in control of your sugar intake. Choose the answer that best describes you.

Behavior Regarding Sugar Consumption

I have tried to reduce my consumption of sweets but failed.
❏ Applies to me ❏ Sometimes ❏ Does not apply to me

The amount of sweets I eat keeps increasing.
❏ Applies to me ❏ Sometimes ❏ Does not apply to me

I often eat more than I planned to.
❏ Applies to me ❏ Sometimes ❏ Does not apply to me

Once I start eating sweets, I can't stop.
❏ Applies to me ❏ Sometimes ❏ Does not apply to me

I can't portion out my sweets; I often eat everything at once.
❏ Applies to me ❏ Sometimes ❏ Does not apply to me

Sometimes I go to the fridge at night to get something sweet.
❏ Applies to me ❏ Sometimes ❏ Does not apply to me

I hide sweets to eat them later, undisturbed or in secret.
❑ Applies to me ❑ Sometimes ❑ Does not apply to me

I always eat everything on my snack plate.
❑ Applies to me ❑ Sometimes ❑ Does not apply to me

Thoughts and Emotions

My thoughts constantly revolve around sweets.
❑ Applies to me ❑ Sometimes ❑ Does not apply to me

I feel controlled by thoughts of sweets.
❑ Applies to me ❑ Sometimes ❑ Does not apply to me

I feel like my well-being depends on how much sweets I eat.
❑ Applies to me ❑ Sometimes ❑ Does not apply to me

I eat sweets even when I'm already full.
❑ Applies to me ❑ Sometimes ❑ Does not apply to me

I perceive my sugar consumption as problematic.
❑ Applies to me ❑ Sometimes ❑ Does not apply to me

I wish I could eat less sugar, but I feel powerless.
❑ Applies to me ❑ Sometimes ❑ Does not apply to me

Physical and Emotional Reactions

I get restless, moody, depressed, or irritated when I go without sweets for a while.
❑ Applies to me ❑ Sometimes ❑ Does not apply to me

I feel restless or tense if I'm not allowed to eat sweets.
❑ Applies to me ❑ Sometimes ❑ Does not apply to me

I notice physical symptoms like headaches when I don't eat sugar.
❑ Applies to me ❑ Sometimes ❑ Does not apply to me

Eating Habits and Control

I follow strict diet plans that divide meals into "allowed" and "forbidden."
❑ Applies to me ❑ Sometimes ❑ Does not apply to me

I feel like sugar calms me down or helps me cope with stress.
❑ Applies to me ❑ Sometimes ❑ Does not apply to me

I often eat sweets out of boredom or frustration.
❑ Applies to me ❑ Sometimes ❑ Does not apply to me

Social Behavior

I cancel meetings or activities to eat sweets.
❑ Applies to me ❑ Sometimes ❑ Does not apply to me

I feel guilty after eating a lot of sweets.
❑ Applies to me ❑ Sometimes ❑ Does not apply to me

Evaluation

Count the number of responses marked as "Applies to me" or "Sometimes." The more of these answers you select, the more likely it is that you may be struggling with your sugar consumption.

Scoring Notes

0–5 points: Your sugar consumption seems to be within normal limits.

6–10 points: It might be helpful to consciously reflect on your sugar consumption.

11+ points: Your behavior may indicate a strong dependency or sugar addiction. Consider seeking professional help or strategies to reduce your sugar consumption.